# BIGHORN SHEEP

Tom Jackson

**Grolier**
an imprint of

www.scholastic.com/librarypublishing

Published 2008 by Grolier
An imprint of Scholastic Library Publishing
Old Sherman Turnpike, Danbury,
Connecticut 06816

**For The Brown Reference Group plc**
Project Editor: Jolyon Goddard
Copy-editors: Lesley Ellis, Lisa Hughes,
    Wendy Horobin
Picture Researcher: Clare Newman
Designers: Jeni Child, Lynne Ross,
    Sarah Williams
Managing Editor: Bridget Giles

Volume ISBN-13: 978-0-7172-6218-2
Volume ISBN-10: 0-7172-6218-9

**Library of Congress
Cataloging-in-Publication Data**

Nature's children. Set 1.
    p. cm.
  Includes index.
  ISBN-13: 978-0-7172-8080-3
  ISBN-10: 0-7172-8080-2 37574349
  1. Animals--Encyclopedias, Juvenile.    5108
  QL49.N38 2007
  590--dc22

                        2007018358

Printed and bound in China

**PICTURE CREDITS**

**Front Cover**: Shutterstock: Ronnie
Howard.

**Back Cover**: Nature PL: Michael Durham;
Shutterstock: Jason Cheever, Ronnie
Howard; Superstock: Age Fotostock.

**Alamy**: Ernesto Burciaga 8; **Corbis**: James
L. Amos 12, W. Perry Conway 28, Darrell
Gulin 41, Steve Kaufman 16, Mary Ann
McDonald 42, Galen Rowell 34; **FLPA**:
Michael Durham/Minden Pictures 37,
Sumio Harada/Minden Pictures 23, 45,
ZSSD/Minden Pictures 4, 7; **PhotoDisc**: Alan
and Sandy Carey 11; **Photolibrary.com**:
Erwin and Peggy Bauer 46, Bob Bennett 2–3,
33, Howie Garber 38, Stouffer Productions
20; **Shutterstock**: Jason Cheever 5, 26–27,
Rick Parsons 15; **Still Pictures**: S. Meyers
30; Superstock: Age Fotostock 19.

# Contents

# FACT FILE: Bighorn Sheep

| | |
|---|---|
| **Class** | Mammals (Mammalia) |
| **Order** | Cloven-hoofed mammals (Artiodactyla) |
| **Family** | Antelope, cattle, sheep, and goats (Bovidae) |
| **Genus** | Sheep (*Ovis*) |
| **Species** | Bighorn sheep (*Ovis canadensis*) |
| **World distribution** | North America |
| **Habitat** | Mountains and hills |
| **Distinctive physical characteristics** | Large curving horns; the male's horns are spiral; the coat is brown |
| **Habits** | Bighorn sheep live in flocks of 10 to 100 animals; bighorns are active in daytime; they make an annual migration |
| **Diet** | Grasses, shrubs, lichens, and the twigs and needles of some trees |

# Introduction

Do you want to climb the Rocky Mountains? To get to the top, you will need some ropes to pull yourself up and special shoes that stop you from slipping. It is very hard work and could take several days. When you reach the high slopes, you'll find that another animal has gotten there before you—equipped with nothing but four sturdy feet. This natural climber is the bighorn sheep, often called the "King of the Mountains." Do not be fooled. Bighorn sheep are not meek and timid like the sheep you see on farms. These wild creatures are fearless and strong. How else do you think they survive on the mountains?

**A bighorn ram takes a rest.**

# Playful Lambs

It must be fun climbing and jumping over rocks all day. Young bighorn sheep certainly think so. They even like to play some games that you might have heard about! The **lambs** play follow the leader. They run after each other along the narrow ledges. Lambs also like to play king of the mountain. One lamb climbs to the top of a pile of rocks. The rest of the gang clamber up and try to knock the lamb off.

These games are not just great fun; they also teach the lambs valuable skills. It makes them into expert climbers who can run and jump safely on steep slopes. That is very important if you are a bighorn sheep.

Bighorn lambs
bound down
a steep hillside.

7

A bighorn ram watches from his mountain home.

# Bighorn Home

Bighorn sheep are not quite as widespread as their white fluffy cousins that live on farms. The type of place, or **habitat**, where bighorn sheep live is in the mountains. The sheep can be found only in the mountains of western North America. Some live as far south as Mexico. But most live farther north in the Rocky Mountains. You are most likely to spot a bighorn sheep on a hike through the mountains of British Columbia and Alberta in southern Canada.

Bighorns like to stay away from people. These sheep live in remote areas of wilderness. In summer the sheep live high up the mountainside. When the snows come in winter, bighorns move down to the valleys.

# Meet the Family

There are seven **species**, or types, of sheep in the world. Together they form the **genus**, or group of related species, *Ovis*. This genus includes the domestic, or farmyard, sheep, *Ovis aries*. However, sheep do not all live on farms. Like the bighorns, most of the seven species are wild animals. Most types of wild sheep live in Asia. That is where the first domestic sheep were raised about 8,000 years ago. North America is the only other place where wild sheep live. As well as the bighorn sheep, the other American species is the thinhorn sheep. The thinhorn sheep is also called Dall's sheep. It lives in much colder places than bighorns. Thinhorns are found in Alaska and the Yukon in Canada.

A fully grown male bighorn, or **ram**, is about 3.5 feet (1 m) tall. It weighs about 340 pounds (155 kg). That is one and a half times bigger than a farm sheep! Female bighorns—the **ewes**—are much smaller than the rams. The females weigh up to 175 pounds (80 kg).

This thinhorn sheep lives in North America, in colder places than its bighorn cousin.

11

A bighorn's wool coat becomes much thicker in winter.

# Where's the Wool?

We are all used to seeing domestic sheep with wool. Wool is a mass of thin curly hairs. It is the stuff we use to make a cozy sweater or to knit a hat. Looking at the coat of a bighorn sheep, it is hard to see why they are called sheep at all. Have the scientists got it right?

The wool is there, it is just shorter than we are used to seeing on farm sheep. The wool is hidden under longer hairs. These longer hairs are called **guard hairs**. They cover the wool and stop it from getting wet in the rain and snow. The curly wool is called **underfur**. The underfur traps little pockets of air. The body warms the pockets of air. That makes the hair work in the same way as a thick blanket. It keeps the sheep warm even in the strong winds at the top of a mountain.

# Sure-footed Sheep

If you tried to run up and down a slippery mountainside and make great leaps between icy ledges, you would not last long. Sooner or later you would slip and probably hurt yourself. That is why human mountain climbers train hard and take great care as they climb. But bighorn sheep do not have the same worries. How do they climb so well?

The key to a bighorn sheep's success is its nonslip feet. The outer edge of each **hoof** is hard and sharp. The sheep use that edge to dig into earth or ice and get a firm grip. The central part of the sheep's foot is covered by a spongy pad. The pad does not slide on the ground easily so it helps grip. The sheep's hoof is split in two. The halves pinch together so they can hold onto rocks. Two claws at the back of each foot dig into the ground if the sheep does slip. That stops the sheep from sliding too far. If a bighorn does fall, it can twist its body around in midair and land on its feet!

The secret of a
bighorn's climbing
success is its
gripping feet.

The bighorn ewe (top) has much smaller horns than those of the ram (below).

# Big Horns

Can you guess how the bighorn sheep got its name? Thought so! It's because of their huge curving **horns**. Both bighorn rams and ewes grow horns. However, only a ram's horns grow into thick curls. A ewe's are thinner and just sweep backward. Unlike the antlers of a deer, a bighorn's headgear does not fall off each year. The horns keep growing throughout its life. Older rams have really huge horns. They can grow to 45 inches (1.2 m) long and weigh 30 pounds (14 kg).

These giant horns are useful in fights. Yet the horns can be a bit of a nuisance for the rams. The horns are very heavy. They can grow so long that they block some of a ram's view. Older rams rub the tips of their horns against a rock to wear them down.

# Super Vision

Bighorn sheep live on the sides of mountains. So **predators** have a tough time sneaking up on the sheep. The sheep can see for miles from a high position. They have very sharp eyes that make the most of a good view. Their large amber-colored eyes can spot things moving 5 miles (8 km) away. A person would need a telescope or a pair of binoculars to see that far!

It is not just a bighorn sheep's eyes that are supersensitive. Bighorns can also hear and smell very well. Those senses are used when it is too dark to see. Together the sheep's eyes, ears, and nose make sure that enemies do not get a chance to get too close.

Bighorns have super
eyesight. Their senses
of smell and hearing
are excellent, too.

A cougar chases a
bighorn ram down
a mountain slope.

# Under Attack!

During summer, bighorn sheep live in the high mountains. There, adults have few enemies. Only the cougar hunts the sheep in the mountains. The lambs are in much greater danger, however, especially from hungry golden eagles. These birds are strong enough to swoop in and snatch a lamb from the ground. If the sheep spot an eagle, the lambs squeeze under their mother's belly. The mothers have no trouble shooing away the eagle with their horns.

In winter the sheep move down to the valleys. There, they have far more enemies. Down in the valley, they are at risk of attack from grizzly bears, coyotes, wolves, and bobcats. Catching a bighorn sheep is far from easy. If a predator manages to get close, the sheep tries to run away. If a sheep is cornered, it turns and charges at the attacker with its horns down. That is enough to frighten off even the hungriest hunter!

# Bighorn Bleaters

Bighorn sheep are different from their farmyard cousins in many ways. But there are some features that are the same. Bighorns bleat just like their cousins.

A mother gives out a low "baa" to call her lamb. That warns the lamb to come close because danger is near. Lambs let their mother know they are hungry with a higher bleat. Bighorn rams do not "baa" very much. They like to snort in a threatening way, especially when they are ready for a fight!

When a bighorn ram snorts, he's ready for a fight!

# Grass Guzzlers

Bighorn sheep are grazers—they eat grass. You might think that a grazer eats all the time. Not this one! Bighorn sheep have three meals a day and some snacks in between, just like you!

The sheep have their first meal of the day as soon as the Sun is up. The menu is always the same: grass! The next meal is at midday. The last meal is in the late afternoon, so the sheep do not get hungry during the night.

The sheep sometimes eat the leaves of shrubs to spice up their diet. But in winter they have to make do with whatever they can find in the snow. They even eat twigs and fir needles!

# Chew, Chew

Have you ever chewed a stalk of straw? It is tough isn't it? It is lucky you are not a bighorn sheep. Tough grass is what they eat every day. The sheep's plant food is so tough that bighorns have to chew food twice!

A bighorn's teeth cannot slice the grass up easily. Instead their teeth grind the food into a paste. This paste is swallowed and travels to the stomach. There it is mixed with juices that begin to digest it, or break it down. Later, when the sheep is relaxing after its meal, the paste, or **cud**, travels back up the sheep's throat and back into the mouth. The sheep gives it a second chew before swallowing the food again. That makes doubly sure the food is broken down enough to be well digested. This process is called chewing the cud.

This bighorn sheep is busy chewing the cud.

# Band Leader

Like other sheep, bighorns live in flocks, or **bands**. A band of bighorns can contain as many as 100 sheep. But most bands are much smaller, with about ten members. In summer when the bighorns are high up in the mountains, the bands split up. Rams live together in bachelor clubs. The ewes and young sheep live in separate groups.

The ram-only bands are led by the toughest member. The sheep figure out which of them is in charge by comparing the size of one another's horns. The ram with the largest horns has lived the longest or grown the fastest, so he becomes the chief. Sometimes another ram challenges the leader. The two rivals sort out who is in charge with a head-butting contest. That might seem dangerous, but the curved horns rarely do any serious damage.

A band of rams rests
on the grassy slopes of
a mountain in Montana.

In summer bighorn ewes form their own bands in the mountains.

# Ewe Chief

While the rams are fighting one another to see who is boss, the ewes stay well away. Any ram that approaches a females' band is chased away. The ewes do not want him causing trouble. They prefer to graze the mountain meadows and relax. Just like the band of rams, a single sheep leads the ewes. She is generally the oldest member of the group. This ewe leads her band through the rocks to find new places to feed. The chief ewe stands guard over the band as the others feed. If she sees something dangerous, such as a cougar, she raises the alarm by stamping a foot. Then, she bolts away, leading the band to a safer position higher up the mountain.

# Into the Valley

When winter comes, the rams and ewes once
again gather in larger bands. They stay in these
mixed groups until spring. In winter the high
mountain slopes are covered in snow. That
makes it difficult for the sheep to find food.
Once snow is on the ground, the bighorns head
down the slope to more sheltered valleys. These
valleys are protected from the icy wind. There
is also less snow at these lower altitudes. A band
of bighorns follows the same route to their
wintering grounds each year. The sheep might
walk 25 miles (40 km) to reach their new home.
The older sheep have been there before, so
they can lead the younger ones. The elders
also lead the way back up to the mountains in
spring. This long journey that the bighorns
make each year is called a **migration**.

In early winter a band of bighorns heads into the valleys, away from the cold mountains.

A bighorn is fast
on its feet. An adult
can also jump up to
7 feet (2 m) high.

# Downward Trek

Migrating bighorns travel in single file. Each band is led by the chief ram. He takes his role very seriously. The chief head-butts any other sheep that try to overtake him. Bighorns are not slow animals. They can run at 35 miles an hour (56 km/h) and jump 7 feet (2 m) into the air. Nevertheless, the ram makes sure that the band does not travel faster than a trot. That ensures everyone can keep up. If the band's path is blocked by a river, the sheep swim across.

The migration can take several days as the sheep pick their way through rugged ground. When it is time for a rest, the sheep lie down together. They tuck their feet under their body to keep warm.

# In the Snow

In winter the days are short and cold. When the Sun is up, it is in the southern part of the sky. Bighorns choose a south-facing slope to spend the winter. This slope gets more warm sunlight on it than other slopes. The bighorns can sunbathe there. The extra warmth quickly melts any snow that falls.

When snow covers the ground, bighorns have trouble finding food. They can use their hooves to scrape away snow, uncovering the grass beneath. But if the snow is very deep, the sheep have to go hungry. During a blizzard, a band gathers in the shelter of an overhanging cliff or in a cave. Life will be a lot easier for the sheep when spring arrives.

Winter is a hard
time for bighorns.
Deep snow makes
it difficult for them
to find grass to eat.

Bighorn rams fight.
The winner gets to
mate with the ewes.

# Taking a Stand

Once a band of bighorns has settled into its winter home, the rams become grouchy with one another. It is now the **mating season**. The rams compete with one another to find ewes to **mate** with.

A ram tries to mate with as many ewes as he can. However, it is not easy. If a ewe in the band becomes ready to mate, several rams try to be her partner. The competing rams size one another up. The older and stronger rams with the largest horns soon chase away the smaller males. A snort and a quick charge with their mighty horns is enough to do that. But all too often, two equally matched rams choose the same female. The two challengers must fight to see who will be her mate.

# Butting Heads

A bighorn battle begins with the rams circling each other about 30 feet (9 m) apart. Suddenly, the challengers both rear up on their hind legs. As their front feet touch the ground they are off at top speed. The rams hurtle toward each other. They lower their head and crash head on. The mighty impact creates a cracking noise that echoes across the mountains.

Both rams are stunned by the blow. They spend a little while shaking their head to drive away dizziness. Then they are back in the ring and ready for the next round. The rams butt heads again and again. The fight might take hours. The rams are seldom hurt because they are protected by their thick skull and strong neck. The skull and neck absorb the force of the blows. The rams must still get headaches, though, don't you think?

Crack! Bighorn rams
head-butt each other.
Their fighting might
go on for hours.

Bighorn sheep shed their thick winter coat, which is replaced by a thin coat in summer.

# All Change

A bighorn sheep's thick winter coat helps it survive cold months. But this fur would be too heavy in summer. As the days become longer and warmer, the sheep's coat changes. The long underfur falls out in clumps. That makes the sheep look a little shaggy and ragged, but it is not going bald. As the longer hairs fall out, a shorter and lighter coat replaces them. This summer coat is more suitable for a season of leaping about the mountain tops.

The process of changing coats is called **molting**. The molt also gives the sheep a paler coat. The process is reversed in fall, when the days become shorter once again. At this time, the sheep's woollen coat thickens, in preparation for the cold winter.

# Born on a Cliff

A bighorn ewe is pregnant for about six months.
She becomes ready to give birth when the band
is still sheltering in the valley. The mother-to-be
leaves the band and looks for somewhere to
give birth. She chooses a sheltered spot, such
as a ledge on a cliff.

Most ewes give birth to a single lamb. The
newborn lamb is wet. The mother licks it dry.
The mother and baby then touch noses. That
way they learn each other's scent. The lamb
is soon able to stand, but it is a bit wobbly
at first. A bighorn lamb is 16 inches (40 cm)
tall. It already has little buttons of bone where
the horns will grow. The lamb nurses, or
suckles, its mother's milk. As it suckles, the
lamb stands cuddled beneath its mother's
legs. The mother makes soothing "baas,"
so her baby can recognize her voice.

A mother ewe and her lamb rest together.

This four-day-old
lamb is already
exploring its
surroundings.

# Climbing High

Mother and lamb return to the main band after a few hours. The younger members of the band crowd around the newborn and welcome it. Sometimes that gets to be too much. So mother and lamb sneak off for a bit of privacy.

The lamb gets stronger by the hour. Just a few days after being born it can run and jump. It is important for the lamb to learn quickly. At less than a month old, the lamb must travel up the mountain with the rest of the band. When spring comes, it will soon be time to go. The climb is long and dangerous. The chief ram leads slowly so straggling lambs can keep up. Otherwise predators such as cougars or coyotes will be feasting on a lamb dinner. The ewes protect their babies from danger. The lambs run to their mothers when they call.

# Coming of Age

Once they reach the mountain slopes, a band of sheep soon splits into groups of rams and ewes. The lambs and the younger sheep stay with their mothers. The snow has melted. The sunny meadows are filled with lush grass. There is plenty of food for all. Gradually, the lambs nurse less and less. They spend most of their time playing games of follow the leader and king of the mountain. The ewes take turns watching the lambs as they play.

By the end of summer, the lambs weigh about 75 pounds (34 kg). By fall it is time to head down to the low country. Then, lambs are ready to look after themselves. They will not be fully grown for another couple of years, though. Even then, the young rams have to wait a few more years before they are strong enough to challenge the chief.

# Words to Know

**Bands**        Groups of bighorn sheep.

**Cud**        Swallowed food that is brought back into the mouth for chewing a second time. Cud is a paste.

**Ewes**        Female sheep.

**Genus**        A group of species that are closely related to one another.

**Guard hairs**        Long coarse hairs that make up the outer layer of a bighorn sheep's coat.

**Habitat**        Type of place a plant or animal lives.

**Hoof**        The foot of a sheep, deer, and many other animals. The hoof like is a giant, thickened fingernail or claw.

**Horns**        Bony outgrowths on the head of sheep and other hoofed animals.

| | |
|---|---|
| **Lamb** | A young sheep. |
| **Mate** | To come together to produce young. |
| **Mating season** | The time of year when animals come together to mate. |
| **Migration** | A long journey made each year to find a place to feed, mate, or give birth. |
| **Molting** | Shedding fur and growing new fur, usually at a change of season. |
| **Predators** | Animals that hunt other animals for food. |
| **Ram** | A male sheep. |
| **Species** | The scientific word for the animals of the same type that breed together. |
| **Underfur** | A thick layer of short hairs that covers the skin and lies under an outer coat of guard hairs. |

# Find Out More

**Books**

Feinstein, S. *The Bighorn Sheep: Help Save this Endangered Species!* Saving Endangered Species. Berkeley Heights, New Jersey: Myreportlinks.com, 2007.

Mattern, J. *Bighorn Sheep.* Wildlife of North America. Mantako, Minnesota: Capstone Press, 2006.

**Web sites**

**Bighorn Facts**
*www.desertusa.com/big.html*
Lots of facts about bighorns.

**Bighorn Sheep**
*www.enchantedlearning.com/subjects/mammals/sheep/Bighornsheep.shtml*
Print out a bighorn to color in.

# Index